My First Prayer Journal

FOR KIDS

A DAILY DEVOTIONAL WITH PROMPTS FOR GRATITUDE, PRAYER, & LEARNING SCRIPTURE

INEL WILLIAMS

W9-BDO-186

Copyright © 2024 Inel williams.
All rights reserved. No part of this book may be reproduced, stored
in a retrieval system, or transmitted in any form or by any means,
electronic, mechanical, photocopying, recording, or otherwise,
without prior written permission of the copyright owner.

THIS JOURNAL
BELONGS TO

_____

_____

HOW TO USE THIS JOURNAL

This journal has 60 days of prompts. Each day is divided into two parts: left and right - or in other words, daytime and evening. The prompts with the dark-colored banners - "Write This Bible Verse" and "Biblical Knowledge" - both may require a bit of research. It is recommended that the Bible and/ or Google be used to answer these.

After giving thanks, each verse should be handwritten to enhance reflection and memorization. Every day ends with reflecting on Jesus, two brief prayers, and a randomized Biblical Knowledge question. Some questions are related to the Bible verse, and some are not. They can serve as a point of discussion between child and adult. Looking up a short, animated YouTube video about a biblical person, place, or event mentioned is recommended in order to increase engagement and understanding.

What was/ is Jesus Like?

Jesus was and is all that is good and holy. He taught us how to do right - in other words, how to be righteous. This is based on treating yourself and others like we are all images of God (Genesis 1:27). This means serving others, and loving both your neighbor and enemy. Instead of just watching our actions - which was the law in the Old Testament - Jesus wants us to take it a step further. He wants us to watch what is in our hearts and minds. Bad thoughts and a hard heart make us sin. So to follow Jesus, we should be mindful of our thoughts, actions, and hearts. This helps us love and respect ourselves and others. Being mindful of this doesn't mean you won't ever sin or make mistakes. We are all sinners. It means you try to learn from Jesus: by being kind, strong, gentle, fair, brave, patient, forgiving, disciplined, selfless, helpful, compassionate and humble.

PRAISE GOD FOR THIS DAY ☀

Today is: Su (M) T W Th F Sa

2 / 17 / 2025

I thank God for...

1. my new shoes.
2. the sunny weather today.
3. my family and those who love me.

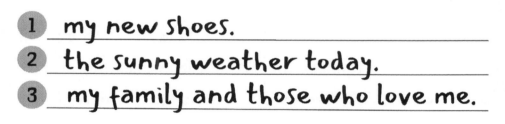

WRITE THIS BIBLE VERSE

DEUTERONOMY 31:6

Be strong and courageous. Don't be afraid nor scared of them; for Yahweh your God Himself is who goes with you. He will not fail you nor forsake you.

Today I tried to be like Jesus by...

loving people even if they don't like me, and turning the other cheek.

A short prayer for someone:

My friend is sick. I pray they feel better. I hope they're not sick for too long.

A short prayer for me:

I pray I do well on my test tomorrow.

BIBLICAL KNOWLEDGE 💡

Why did Mary, Joseph, and baby Jesus flee from Bethlehem to Egypt?

They fled so Jesus would be safe from King Herod. Herod didn't like that Jesus was going to be King one day.

PRAISE GOD FOR THIS DAY ☀

Today is: Su M T W Th F Sa

____ / ____ / _____

I thank God for...

1 _____

2 _____

3 _____

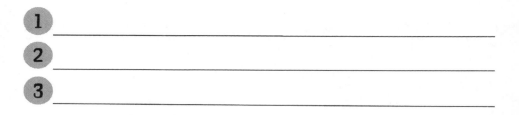

WRITE THIS BIBLE VERSE

PROVERBS 19:8

_____

_____

_____

_____

_____

BLESSED BE THIS EVENING 🌙

Today I tried to be like Jesus by...

_____

A short prayer for someone:

_____

A short prayer for me:

_____

BIBLICAL KNOWLEDGE 💡

What are two things Jesus taught in His famous Sermon on the Mount?

_____

_____

_____

_____

PRAISE GOD FOR THIS DAY ☀

Today is: Su   M   T   W   Th   F   Sa

____ / ____ / _____

I thank God for...

1 _____

2 _____

3 _____

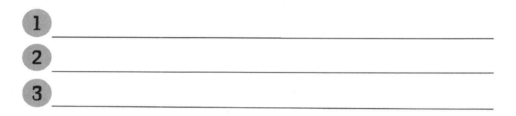

WRITE THIS BIBLE VERSE

ROMANS 3:23

_____

_____

_____

_____

_____

_____

BLESSED BE THIS EVENING 🌙

Today I tried to be like Jesus by...

_____

A short prayer for someone:

_____

A short prayer for me:

_____

BIBLICAL KNOWLEDGE 💡

Which man was thrown into a den of lions but survived unharmed because of his faith? Who ordered him to be thrown into the lion's den?

_____

_____

_____

_____

4

PRAISE GOD FOR THIS DAY

Today is: Su   M   T   W   Th   F   Sa

____ / ____ / _____

I thank God for...

1 _____

2 _____

3 _____

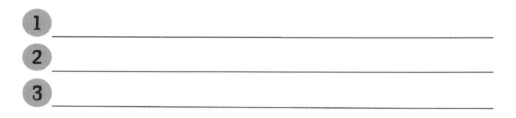

WRITE THIS BIBLE VERSE

GALATIANS 3:28

_____

_____

_____

_____

_____

_____

_____

BLESSED BE THIS EVENING 🌙

Today I tried to be like Jesus by...

_____

A short prayer for someone:

_____

A short prayer for me:

_____

BIBLICAL KNOWLEDGE 💡

What was the name of the man who was sold into slavery by his jealous brothers? What role did he later play in Egypt?

_____
_____
_____
_____

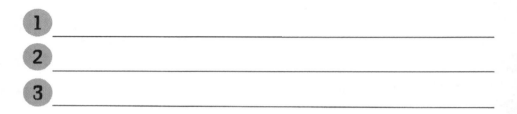

PRAISE GOD FOR THIS DAY ☀

Today is: Su   M   T   W   Th   F   Sa

___ / ___ / _____

I thank God for...

1 _____

2 _____

3 _____

WRITE THIS BIBLE VERSE

JOHN 4:7-8

_____

_____

_____

_____

_____

_____

BLESSED BE THIS EVENING 🌙

Today I tried to be like Jesus by...

_____

A short prayer for someone:

_____

A short prayer for me:

_____

BIBLICAL KNOWLEDGE 💡

Which man spent three days and nights in the belly of a big fish? What did God tell him to say to the people in Nineveh?

_____

_____

_____

_____

PRAISE GOD FOR THIS DAY

Today is: Su M T W Th F Sa

_____ / _____ / _____

I thank God for...

1 _____

2 _____

3 _____

WRITE THIS BIBLE VERSE

1 PETER 5:7

_____

_____

_____

_____

_____

_____

Today I tried to be like Jesus by...

_____

A short prayer for someone:

_____

A short prayer for me:

_____

BIBLICAL KNOWLEDGE 💡

What lesson did Jesus teach with His Parable of the Good Samaritan?

_____

_____

_____

_____

PRAISE GOD FOR THIS DAY ☀

Today is: Su   M   T   W   Th   F   Sa

_____ / _____ / _____

I thank God for...

1 _____

2 _____

3 _____

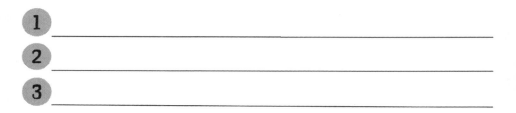

WRITE THIS BIBLE VERSE

NUMBERS 6:24-26

_____

_____

_____

_____

_____

_____

Today I tried to be like Jesus by...

_____

A short prayer for someone:

_____

A short prayer for me:

_____

BIBLICAL KNOWLEDGE 💡

In Genesis, what two cities were destroyed? Why were they destroyed?

_____

_____

_____

_____

PRAISE GOD FOR THIS DAY

Today is: Su M T W Th F Sa

_____ / _____ / _____

I thank God for...

1 _____

2 _____

3 _____

WRITE THIS BIBLE VERSE

PHILIPPIANS 4:13

_____

_____

_____

_____

_____

_____

_____

BLESSED BE THIS EVENING 🌙

Today I tried to be like Jesus by...

_____

A short prayer for someone:

_____

A short prayer for me:

_____

BIBLICAL KNOWLEDGE 💡

What is a covenant? There are five big covenants God made in the Bible. Name the five people with whom God made these covenants.

_____

_____

_____

_____

PRAISE GOD FOR THIS DAY

Today is: Su M T W Th F Sa

____ / ____ / _____

I thank God for...

1 _____

2 _____

3 _____

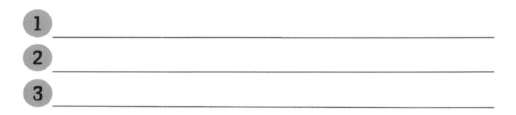

WRITE THIS BIBLE VERSE

HEBREWS 13:8

_____

_____

_____

_____

_____

_____

_____

BLESSED BE THIS EVENING 🌙

Today I tried to be like Jesus by...

_____

A short prayer for someone:

_____

A short prayer for me:

_____

BIBLICAL KNOWLEDGE 💡

How many books are in the New Testament? How about the Old Testament? How many books make up the Bible in total?

_____

_____

_____

_____

Today is: Su M T W Th F Sa

____ / ____ / _____

I thank God for...

1 _____

2 _____

3 _____

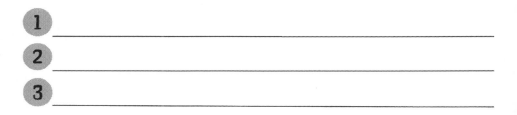

WRITE THIS BIBLE VERSE

EXODUS 20:2-3

_____

_____

_____

_____

_____

_____

_____

BLESSED BE THIS EVENING 🌙

Today I tried to be like Jesus by...

_____

A short prayer for someone:

_____

A short prayer for me:

_____

BIBLICAL KNOWLEDGE 💡

List all of the Ten Commandments.

_____

_____

_____

_____

PRAISE GOD FOR THIS DAY

Today is: Su   M   T   W   Th   F   Sa

____ / ____ / _____

I thank God for...

1 _____

2 _____

3 _____

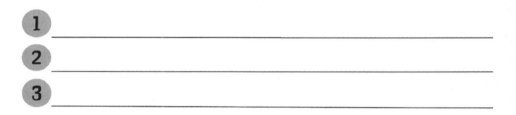

EPHESIANS 4:32

_____

_____

_____

_____

_____

_____

BLESSED BE THIS EVENING 🌙

Today I tried to be like Jesus by...

_____

A short prayer for someone:

_____

A short prayer for me:

_____

BIBLICAL KNOWLEDGE 💡

Who did Jacob wrestle with? What new name was Jacob given after wrestling? What does his new name mean?

_____

_____

_____

_____

PRAISE GOD FOR THIS DAY

Today is: Su   M   T   W   Th   F   Sa

____ / ____ / _____

I thank God for...

1 _____

2 _____

3 _____

WRITE THIS BIBLE VERSE

JOB 1:21

_____

_____

_____

_____

_____

_____

BLESSED BE THIS EVENING 🌙

Today I tried to be like Jesus by...

_____

A short prayer for someone:

_____

A short prayer for me:

_____

BIBLICAL KNOWLEDGE 💡

What did Job lose? Did Job lose faith in God after losing these things?

_____

_____

_____

_____

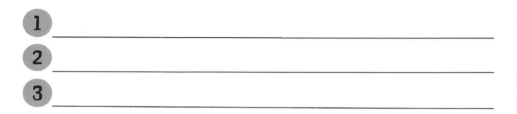

PRAISE GOD FOR THIS DAY

Today is: Su M T W Th F Sa

____ / ____ / _____

I thank God for...

1 _____

2 _____

3 _____

WRITE THIS BIBLE VERSE

1 TIMOTHY 6:12

_____

_____

_____

_____

_____

_____

BLESSED BE THIS EVENING 🌙

Today I tried to be like Jesus by...

_____

A short prayer for someone:

_____

A short prayer for me:

_____

BIBLICAL KNOWLEDGE 💡

Which disciple is known for doubting that Jesus rose from the dead until he saw Him? What did this disciple say when he finally believed?

_____

_____

_____

_____

24

Today is: Su   M   T   W   Th   F   Sa

_____ / _____ / _____

I thank God for...

1 _____

2 _____

3 _____

WRITE THIS BIBLE VERSE

MARK 10:27

_____

_____

_____

_____

_____

_____

_____

BLESSED BE THIS EVENING 🌙

Today I tried to be like Jesus by...

_____

A short prayer for someone:

_____

A short prayer for me:

_____

BIBLICAL KNOWLEDGE 💡

Pharaoh's army was destroyed so Moses and the Israelites could escape. What destroyed Pharaoh's army?

_____
_____
_____
_____

PRAISE GOD FOR THIS DAY ☀

Today is: Su M T W Th F Sa

_____ / _____ / _____

I thank God for...

1 _____

2 _____

3 _____

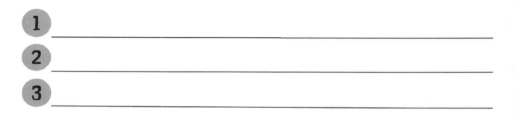

WRITE THIS BIBLE VERSE

PROVERBS 17:17

_____

_____

_____

_____

_____

_____

_____

BLESSED BE THIS EVENING 🌙

Today I tried to be like Jesus by...

_____

A short prayer for someone:

_____

A short prayer for me:

_____

BIBLICAL KNOWLEDGE 💡

How old were Abraham and Sarah when God blessed them with a child? What was the child's name?

_____

_____

_____

_____

PRAISE GOD FOR THIS DAY

Today is: Su M T W Th F Sa

____ / ____ / _____

I thank God for...

1 _____

2 _____

3 _____

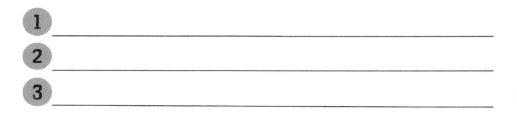

WRITE THIS BIBLE VERSE

ISAIAH 40:31

_____

_____

_____

_____

_____

_____

Today I tried to be like Jesus by...

_____

A short prayer for someone:

_____

A short prayer for me:

_____

BIBLICAL KNOWLEDGE 💡

What was the name of the man who betrayed Jesus with a kiss? What payment did he receive for his betrayal?

_____

_____

_____

_____

PRAISE GOD FOR THIS DAY

Today is: Su M T W Th F Sa

____ / ____ / _____

I thank God for...

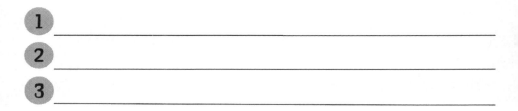

1 _____

2 _____

3 _____

WRITE THIS BIBLE VERSE

LEVITICUS 19:18

BLESSED BE THIS EVENING 🌙

Today I tried to be like Jesus by...

_____

A short prayer for someone:

_____

A short prayer for me:

_____

BIBLICAL KNOWLEDGE 💡

Who was the judge of Israel known for his great strength?
What was the source of his strength?

_____
_____
_____
_____

PRAISE GOD FOR THIS DAY

Today is: Su   M   T   W   Th   F   Sa

_____ / _____ / _____

I thank God for...

1 _____

2 _____

3 _____

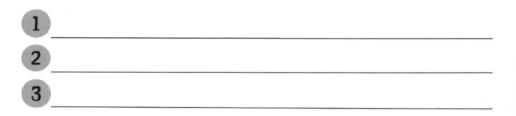

WRITE THIS BIBLE VERSE

LUKE 6:31

_____

_____

_____

_____

_____

_____

_____

BLESSED BE THIS EVENING 🌙

Today I tried to be like Jesus by...

_____

A short prayer for someone:

_____

A short prayer for me:

_____

BIBLICAL KNOWLEDGE 💡

Who was the leader of the Israelites after Moses? What river did he lead them across to enter the Promised Land?

_____

_____

_____

_____

PRAISE GOD FOR THIS DAY

Today is: Su M T W Th F Sa

____ / ____ / _____

I thank God for...

1 _____

2 _____

3 _____

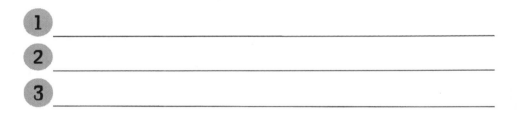

WRITE THIS BIBLE VERSE

MATTHEW 11:28

_____

_____

_____

_____

_____

_____

BLESSED BE THIS EVENING 🌙

Today I tried to be like Jesus by...

_____

A short prayer for someone:

_____

A short prayer for me:

_____

BIBLICAL KNOWLEDGE 💡

What was the name of the King of Israel who defeated a giant?
What was the name of the giant? How was he defeated?

_____

_____

_____

_____

Today is: Su M T W Th F Sa

____ / ____ / _____

I thank God for...

1 _____

2 _____

3 _____

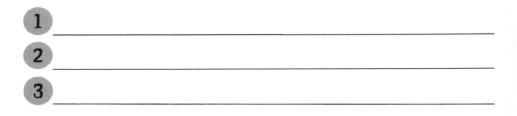

WRITE THIS BIBLE VERSE

1 THESSALONIANS 5:11

_____

_____

_____

_____

_____

_____

_____

BLESSED BE THIS EVENING 🌙

Today I tried to be like Jesus by...

_____

A short prayer for someone:

_____

A short prayer for me:

_____

BIBLICAL KNOWLEDGE 💡

What does resurrection mean? Who was the first person to see Jesus after He was resurrected? Who was Jesus mistaken for?

_____

_____

_____

_____

PRAISE GOD FOR THIS DAY

Today is: Su M T W Th F Sa

____ / ____ / _____

I thank God for...

1 _____

2 _____

3 _____

WRITE THIS BIBLE VERSE

EZEKIEL 36:26

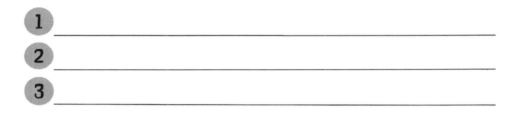

_____

_____

_____

_____

_____

_____

_____

BLESSED BE THIS EVENING 🌙

Today I tried to be like Jesus by...

_____

_____

A short prayer for someone:

_____

_____

A short prayer for me:

_____

_____

BIBLICAL KNOWLEDGE 💡

Who said this quote on the left? Who did they say it to?

_____

_____

_____

_____

_____

PRAISE GOD FOR THIS DAY

Today is: Su M T W Th F Sa

____ / ____ / _____

I thank God for...

1 _____

2 _____

3 _____

WRITE THIS BIBLE VERSE

REVELATION 4:8

_____

_____

_____

_____

_____

_____

BLESSED BE THIS EVENING 🌙

Today I tried to be like Jesus by...

_____

A short prayer for someone:

_____

A short prayer for me:

_____

BIBLICAL KNOWLEDGE 💡

The creatures mentioned in Revelation 4:8 are a type of angel called cherubim. What are two other types of angels?

_____

_____

_____

_____

PRAISE GOD FOR THIS DAY

Today is: Su M T W Th F Sa

____ / ____ / _____

I thank God for...

1 _____

2 _____

3 _____

WRITE THIS BIBLE VERSE

PSALMS 18:1-2

_____

_____

_____

_____

_____

_____

BLESSED BE THIS EVENING 🌙

Today I tried to be like Jesus by...

_____

A short prayer for someone:

_____

A short prayer for me:

_____

BIBLICAL KNOWLEDGE 💡

What mountain did Moses climb? What was Moses given on that mountain? Who gave it to him?

_____

_____

_____

_____

PRAISE GOD FOR THIS DAY

Today is: Su M T W Th F Sa

_____ / _____ / _____

I thank God for...

1 _____

2 _____

3 _____

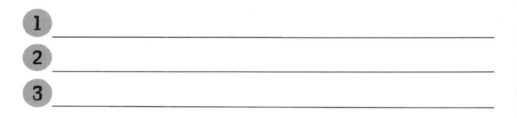

WRITE THIS BIBLE VERSE

EXODUS 20:12

_____

_____

_____

_____

_____

_____

BLESSED BE THIS EVENING 🌙

Today I tried to be like Jesus by...

_____

A short prayer for someone:

_____

A short prayer for me:

_____

BIBLICAL KNOWLEDGE 💡

How are King David and King Solomon related? Which people did they rule over?

_____

_____

_____

_____

PRAISE GOD FOR THIS DAY

Today is: Su M T W Th F Sa

____ / ____ / _____

I thank God for...

1 _____

2 _____

3 _____

WRITE THIS BIBLE VERSE

DANIEL 1:8

_____

_____

_____

_____

_____

_____

BLESSED BE THIS EVENING 🌙

Today I tried to be like Jesus by...

_____

A short prayer for someone:

_____

A short prayer for me:

_____

BIBLICAL KNOWLEDGE 💡

Why wouldn't Daniel eat the food nor drink the wine from the King of Babylon?

_____

_____

_____

_____

PRAISE GOD FOR THIS DAY

Today is: Su M T W Th F Sa

____ / ____ / _____

I thank God for...

1 _____

2 _____

3 _____

WRITE THIS BIBLE VERSE

RUTH 1:16

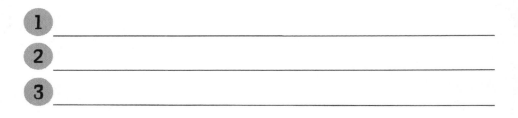

_____
_____
_____
_____
_____
_____

BLESSED BE THIS EVENING 🌙

Today I tried to be like Jesus by...

_____

A short prayer for someone:

_____

A short prayer for me:

_____

BIBLICAL KNOWLEDGE 💡

What is the name of the person Ruth said this to in Ruth 1:16?
How are Ruth and this person related?

_____

_____

_____

_____

PRAISE GOD FOR THIS DAY

Today is: Su   M   T   W   Th   F   Sa

_____ / _____ / _____

I thank God for...

1 _____

2 _____

3 _____

WRITE THIS BIBLE VERSE

PROVERBS 10:19

_____

_____

_____

_____

_____

_____

BLESSED BE THIS EVENING 🌙

Today I tried to be like Jesus by...

_____

A short prayer for someone:

_____

A short prayer for me:

_____

BIBLICAL KNOWLEDGE 💡

What are the names of Jesus' twelve disciples?

_____

_____

_____

_____

Today is: Su M T W Th F Sa

_____ / _____ / _____

I thank God for...

1 _____

2 _____

3 _____

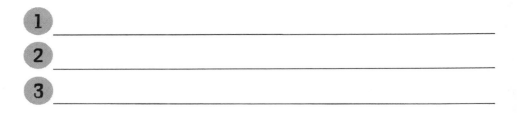

WRITE THIS BIBLE VERSE

GENESIS 9:14-15

_____

_____

_____

_____

_____

_____

BLESSED BE THIS EVENING 🌙

Today I tried to be like Jesus by...

_____

A short prayer for someone:

_____

A short prayer for me:

_____

BIBLICAL KNOWLEDGE 💡

Who is talking here? Who are they talking to? What are they
promising not to do again?

_____

_____

_____

_____

PRAISE GOD FOR THIS DAY

Today is: Su M T W Th F Sa

____ / ____ / _____

I thank God for...

1 _____

2 _____

3 _____

WRITE THIS BIBLE VERSE

DEUTERONOMY 6:5

_____

_____

_____

_____

_____

_____

BLESSED BE THIS EVENING 🌙

Today I tried to be like Jesus by...

_____

A short prayer for someone:

_____

A short prayer for me:

_____

BIBLICAL KNOWLEDGE 💡

Which person was saved before Sodom was destroyed? Who asked God to save the few good people in Sodom?

_____

_____

_____

_____

PRAISE GOD FOR THIS DAY

Today is: Su M T W Th F Sa

____ / ____ / _____

I thank God for...

1 _____

2 _____

3 _____

WRITE THIS BIBLE VERSE

ISAIAH 43:2

_____

_____

_____

_____

_____

_____

_____

BLESSED BE THIS EVENING 🌙

Today I tried to be like Jesus by...

_____

A short prayer for someone:

_____

A short prayer for me:

_____

BIBLICAL KNOWLEDGE 💡

What does the name Abraham mean? What was Abraham's name before it was changed to Abraham?

_____

_____

_____

_____

Today is: Su M T W Th F Sa

____ / ____ / _____

I thank God for...

1 _____

2 _____

3 _____

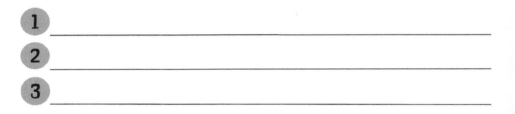

WRITE THIS BIBLE VERSE

2 SAMUEL 22:31

_____

_____

_____

_____

_____

_____

BLESSED BE THIS EVENING 🌙

Today I tried to be like Jesus by...

_____

A short prayer for someone:

_____

A short prayer for me:

_____

BIBLICAL KNOWLEDGE 💡

Paul the Apostle used to dislike Christians. What did Paul's name used to be? What happened to make him become Christian?

_____

_____

_____

_____

PRAISE GOD FOR THIS DAY

Today is: Su   M   T   W   Th   F   Sa

____ / ____ / _____

I thank God for...

1 _____

2 _____

3 _____

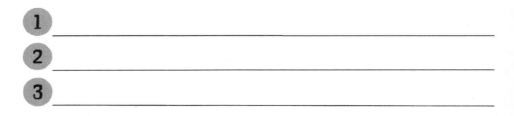

WRITE THIS BIBLE VERSE

2 CORINTHIANS 3:17

_____

_____

_____

_____

_____

_____

BLESSED BE THIS EVENING 🌙

Today I tried to be like Jesus by...

_____

A short prayer for someone:

_____

A short prayer for me:

_____

BIBLICAL KNOWLEDGE 💡

Which King of Israel was Jezebel's husband? What is one sin that Jezebel committed?

_____

_____

_____

_____

PRAISE GOD FOR THIS DAY ☀

Today is: Su   M   T   W   Th   F   Sa

____ / ____ / _____

I thank God for...

1 _____

2 _____

3 _____

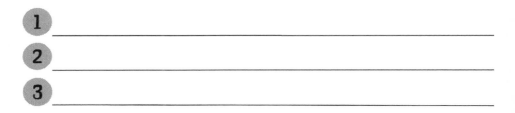

WRITE THIS BIBLE VERSE

JOHN 15:13

_____

_____

_____

_____

_____

_____

Today I tried to be like Jesus by...

_____

A short prayer for someone:

_____

A short prayer for me:

_____

BIBLICAL KNOWLEDGE 💡

What are two examples of deep friendship in the Bible?

_____

_____

_____

_____

PRAISE GOD FOR THIS DAY

Today is: Su M T W Th F Sa

____ / ____ / _____

I thank God for...

1 _____

2 _____

3 _____

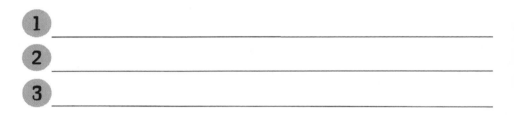

WRITE THIS BIBLE VERSE

MALACHI 3:10

_____

_____

_____

_____

_____

_____

_____

BLESSED BE THIS EVENING 🌙

Today I tried to be like Jesus by...

_____

A short prayer for someone:

_____

A short prayer for me:

_____

BIBLICAL KNOWLEDGE 💡

The person who wrote the Book of Proverbs was the wisest person in the world. Who wrote it? Who wrote the Book of Psalms?

_____

_____

_____

_____

PRAISE GOD FOR THIS DAY

Today is: Su   M   T   W   Th   F   Sa

____ / ____ / _____

I thank God for...

1 _____

2 _____

3 _____

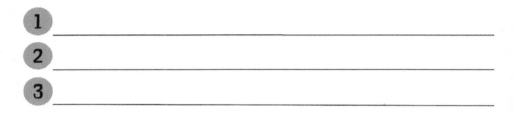
WRITE THIS BIBLE VERSE

HABAKKUK 3:17-18

_____

_____

_____

_____

_____

_____

_____

BLESSED BE THIS EVENING 🌙

Today I tried to be like Jesus by...

_____

A short prayer for someone:

_____

A short prayer for me:

_____

BIBLICAL KNOWLEDGE 💡

Who were the only three people who were both a prophet and a judge of Israel?

_____

_____

_____

_____

PRAISE GOD FOR THIS DAY

Today is: Su M T W Th F Sa

_____ / _____ / _____

I thank God for...

1 _____

2 _____

3 _____

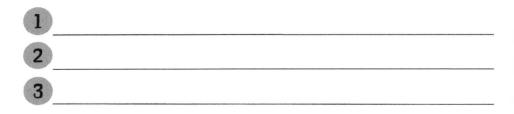

WRITE THIS BIBLE VERSE

JEREMIAH 17:7-8

_____

_____

_____

_____

_____

_____

BLESSED BE THIS EVENING 🌙

Today I tried to be like Jesus by...

_____

A short prayer for someone:

_____

A short prayer for me:

_____

BIBLICAL KNOWLEDGE 💡

What was the name of the person who baptized Jesus? How were they related to Jesus?

_____

_____

_____

_____

PRAISE GOD FOR THIS DAY

Today is: Su M T W Th F Sa

____ / ____ / _____

I thank God for...

1 _____

2 _____

3 _____

WRITE THIS BIBLE VERSE

JAMES 1:2-3

_____

_____

_____

_____

_____

_____

BLESSED BE THIS EVENING 🌙

Today I tried to be like Jesus by...

_____

A short prayer for someone:

_____

A short prayer for me:

_____

BIBLICAL KNOWLEDGE 💡

The Torah is the first part of the Jewish Bible. It is the first five books of the Old Testament. What are the five names of these books?

_____

_____

_____

_____

Today is: Su M T W Th F Sa

____ / ____ / _____

I thank God for...

1 _____

2 _____

3 _____

WRITE THIS BIBLE VERSE

NAHUM 1:7

_____

_____

_____

_____

_____

_____

BLESSED BE THIS EVENING 🌙

Today I tried to be like Jesus by...

_____

A short prayer for someone:

_____

A short prayer for me:

_____

BIBLICAL KNOWLEDGE 💡

Name all of the twelve tribes of Israel (Jacob). Why did the Israelites go to Egypt?

_____

_____

_____

_____

Today is: Su   M   T   W   Th   F   Sa

____ / ____ / _____

I thank God for...

1 _____

2 _____

3 _____

WRITE THIS BIBLE VERSE

2 JOHN 1:6

_____

_____

_____

_____

_____

_____

BLESSED BE THIS EVENING 🌙

Today I tried to be like Jesus by...

_____

A short prayer for someone:

_____

A short prayer for me:

_____

BIBLICAL KNOWLEDGE 💡

What are at least two other names for Jesus mentioned in the Bible? What languages did Jesus speak on Earth?

_____

_____

_____

_____

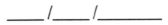

PRAISE GOD FOR THIS DAY

Today is: Su M T W Th F Sa

_____ / _____ / _____

I thank God for...

1 _____

2 _____

3 _____

WRITE THIS BIBLE VERSE

PROVERBS 15:1

_____

_____

_____

_____

_____

_____

_____

BLESSED BE THIS EVENING 🌙

Today I tried to be like Jesus by...

_____

A short prayer for someone:

_____

A short prayer for me:

_____

BIBLICAL KNOWLEDGE 💡

Who visited Jesus' tomb after He was crucified and buried?
What did they find?

_____

_____

_____

_____

Today is: Su   M   T   W   Th   F   Sa

____ / ____ / _____

I thank God for...

1 _____

2 _____

3 _____

WRITE THIS BIBLE VERSE

ECCLESIATES 11:4

_____

_____

_____

_____

_____

_____

_____

BLESSED BE THIS EVENING 🌙

Today I tried to be like Jesus by...

_____

A short prayer for someone:

_____

A short prayer for me:

_____

BIBLICAL KNOWLEDGE 💡

What does it mean to be righteous? Give two examples of what Jesus considers righteous.

_____

_____

_____

_____

PRAISE GOD FOR THIS DAY

Today is: Su M T W Th F Sa

____ / ____ / _____

I thank God for...

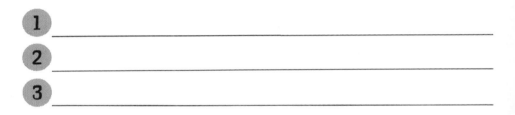

1 _____

2 _____

3 _____

WRITE THIS BIBLE VERSE

PSALMS 23:4

_____

_____

_____

_____

_____

_____

BLESSED BE THIS EVENING 🌙

Today I tried to be like Jesus by...

_____

A short prayer for someone:

_____

A short prayer for me:

_____

BIBLICAL KNOWLEDGE 💡

What is another name for Satan? Why did God throw Satan out of Heaven?

_____

_____

_____

_____

PRAISE GOD FOR THIS DAY

Today is: Su M T W Th F Sa

____ / ____ / _____

I thank God for...

1 _____

2 _____

3 _____

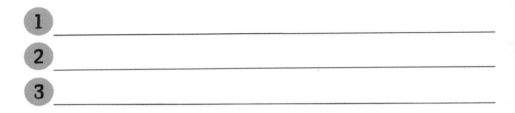

WRITE THIS BIBLE VERSE

MATTHEW 5:38-39

_____

_____

_____

_____

_____

_____

BLESSED BE THIS EVENING 🌙

Today I tried to be like Jesus by...

_____

A short prayer for someone:

_____

A short prayer for me:

_____

BIBLICAL KNOWLEDGE 💡

Which Roman Emperor caused Jesus to be crucified? What part of his body did the Emperor wash before Jesus was crucified? Why?

_____

_____

_____

_____

PRAISE GOD FOR THIS DAY ☀

Today is: Su   M   T   W   Th   F   Sa

_____ / _____ / _____

I thank God for...

1 _____

2 _____

3 _____

WRITE THIS BIBLE VERSE

AMOS 5:24

_____

_____

_____

_____

_____

_____

_____

BLESSED BE THIS EVENING 🌙

Today I tried to be like Jesus by...

_____

A short prayer for someone:

_____

A short prayer for me:

_____

BIBLICAL KNOWLEDGE 💡

What is The Last Supper? In what city did it happen?

_____

_____

_____

_____

PRAISE GOD FOR THIS DAY

Today is: Su M T W Th F Sa

____ / ____ / _____

I thank God for...

1 _____

2 _____

3 _____

WRITE THIS BIBLE VERSE

ROMANS 12:19

_____

_____

_____

_____

_____

_____

_____

BLESSED BE THIS EVENING 🌙

Today I tried to be like Jesus by...

_____

A short prayer for someone:

_____

A short prayer for me:

_____

BIBLICAL KNOWLEDGE 💡

What did Rahab do that pleased God, and made the Israelites accept her? What is the name of Rahab's son?

_____

_____

_____

_____

PRAISE GOD FOR THIS DAY

Today is: Su M T W Th F Sa

____ / ____ / _____

I thank God for...

1 _____

2 _____

3 _____

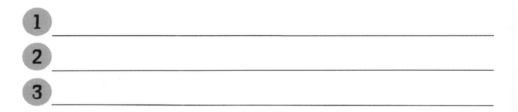

WRITE THIS BIBLE VERSE

ISAIAH 1:17

_____

_____

_____

_____

_____

_____

_____

BLESSED BE THIS EVENING 🌙

Today I tried to be like Jesus by...

_____

A short prayer for someone:

_____

A short prayer for me:

_____

BIBLICAL KNOWLEDGE 💡

The Book of Judges is about the sins of the Israelites, and the sins of their 12 leaders, or judges. Name all twelve of these Israelite judges.

_____

_____

_____

_____

PRAISE GOD FOR THIS DAY ☀

Today is: Su   M   T   W   Th   F   Sa

____ / ____ / _____

I thank God for...

1 _____

2 _____

3 _____

WRITE THIS BIBLE VERSE

2 CORINTHIANS 5:7

_____

_____

_____

_____

_____

_____

_____

Today I tried to be like Jesus by...

_____

A short prayer for someone:

_____

A short prayer for me:

_____

BIBLICAL KNOWLEDGE 💡

Who was the first King of Israel? Who was the second King? The third? The fourth?

_____

_____

_____

_____

PRAISE GOD FOR THIS DAY

Today is: Su M T W Th F Sa

___ / ___ / _____

I thank God for...

1 _____

2 _____

3 _____

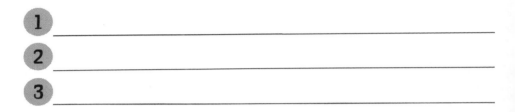

WRITE THIS BIBLE VERSE

MATTHEW 7:7

_____

_____

_____

_____

_____

_____

_____

BLESSED BE THIS EVENING 🌙

Today I tried to be like Jesus by...

_____

A short prayer for someone:

_____

A short prayer for me:

_____

BIBLICAL KNOWLEDGE 💡

King David is related to Jesus by blood. He is Jesus' ancestor. What did God promise David about Jesus and his future kingdom?

_____

_____

_____

_____

PRAISE GOD FOR THIS DAY

Today is: Su   M   T   W   Th   F   Sa

____ / ____ / _____

I thank God for...

1 _____

2 _____

3 _____

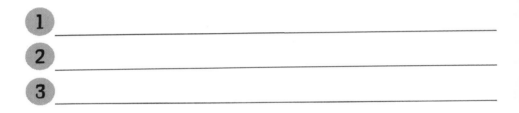

NEHEMIAH 8:10

_____

_____

_____

_____

_____

_____

_____

BLESSED BE THIS EVENING 🌙

Today I tried to be like Jesus by...

_____

A short prayer for someone:

_____

A short prayer for me:

_____

BIBLICAL KNOWLEDGE 💡

What was the name of the Jewish Queen of Persia? What did she do to become a hero?

_____

_____

_____

_____

PRAISE GOD FOR THIS DAY

Today is: Su M T W Th F Sa

____ / ____ / _____

I thank God for...

1 _____

2 _____

3 _____

WRITE THIS BIBLE VERSE

JAMES 1:22

_____

_____

_____

_____

_____

_____

_____

BLESSED BE THIS EVENING 🌙

Today I tried to be like Jesus by...

_____

A short prayer for someone:

_____

A short prayer for me:

_____

BIBLICAL KNOWLEDGE 💡

Who famously asked God, "Am I my brother's keeper"? Why did he ask God this? What was his parents' names?

_____

_____

_____

_____

PRAISE GOD FOR THIS DAY

Today is: Su   M   T   W   Th   F   Sa

_____ / _____ / _____

I thank God for...

1 _____

2 _____

3 _____

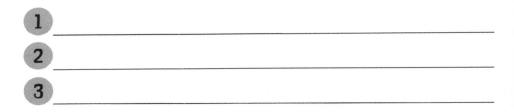

WRITE THIS BIBLE VERSE

PROVERBS 18:24

_____

_____

_____

_____

_____

_____

_____

99

BLESSED BE THIS EVENING 🌙

Today I tried to be like Jesus by...

_____

A short prayer for someone:

_____

A short prayer for me:

_____

BIBLICAL KNOWLEDGE 💡

When Mary and Joseph couldn't find Jesus when He was a child, where did they finally find Him? What did He say to them?

_____

_____

_____

_____

PRAISE GOD FOR THIS DAY ☀

Today is: Su   M   T   W   Th   F   Sa

____ / ____ / _____

I thank God for...

1 _____

2 _____

3 _____

WRITE THIS BIBLE VERSE

ACTS 20:35

_____

_____

_____

_____

_____

_____

BLESSED BE THIS EVENING 🌙

Today I tried to be like Jesus by...

_____

A short prayer for someone:

_____

A short prayer for me:

_____

BIBLICAL KNOWLEDGE 💡

What forgiving sentence did Jesus say while he was being crucified?

_____

_____

_____

_____

Today is: Su   M   T   W   Th   F   Sa

____ / ____ / _____

I thank God for...

1 _____

2 _____

3 _____

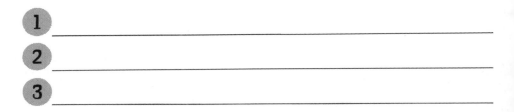

WRITE THIS BIBLE VERSE

GALATIANS 5:22-23

_____
_____
_____
_____
_____
_____

BLESSED BE THIS EVENING 🌙

Today I tried to be like Jesus by...

_____

A short prayer for someone:

_____

A short prayer for me:

_____

BIBLICAL KNOWLEDGE 💡

What was King Saul's downfall according to the prophet Samuel?

_____

_____

_____

_____

PRAISE GOD FOR THIS DAY

Today is: Su M T W Th F Sa

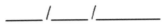

____/____/_____

I thank God for...

1 _____

2 _____

3 _____

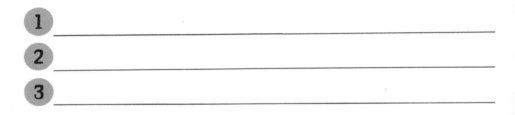

WRITE THIS BIBLE VERSE

1 JOHN 1:9

_____
_____
_____
_____
_____
_____

BLESSED BE THIS EVENING 🌙

Today I tried to be like Jesus by...

_____

A short prayer for someone:

_____

A short prayer for me:

_____

BIBLICAL KNOWLEDGE 💡

Was Mary rich or poor when God chose her to be the mother of Jesus? Was she well-known or not?

_____

_____

_____

_____

PRAISE GOD FOR THIS DAY

Today is: Su   M   T   W   Th   F   Sa

_____ / _____ / _____

I thank God for...

1 _____

2 _____

3 _____

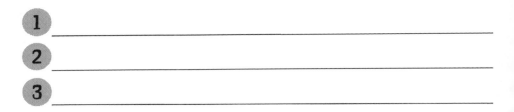

WRITE THIS BIBLE VERSE

1 TIMOTHY 4:12

_____

_____

_____

_____

_____

_____

BLESSED BE THIS EVENING 🌙

Today I tried to be like Jesus by...

_____

A short prayer for someone:

_____

A short prayer for me:

_____

BIBLICAL KNOWLEDGE 💡

What does the word gospel mean? What is the gospel of Jesus?

_____

_____

_____

_____

Today is: Su   M   T   W   Th   F   Sa

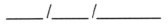

_____ / _____ / _____

I thank God for...

1 _____

2 _____

3 _____

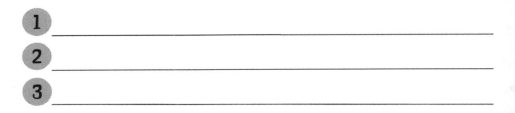

WRITE THIS BIBLE VERSE

ECCLESIASTES 7:20

_____

_____

_____

_____

_____

_____

_____

BLESSED BE THIS EVENING 🌙

Today I tried to be like Jesus by...

_____

A short prayer for someone:

_____

A short prayer for me:

_____

BIBLICAL KNOWLEDGE 💡

What food did Jesus say is His body? What drink did Jesus say is His blood?

_____

_____

_____

_____

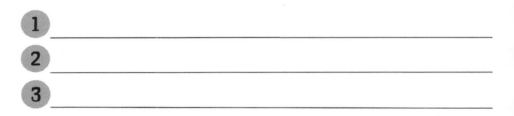

PRAISE GOD FOR THIS DAY

Today is: Su M T W Th F Sa

_____ / _____ / _____

I thank God for...

1 _____

2 _____

3 _____

WRITE THIS BIBLE VERSE

LUKE 15:7

_____

_____

_____

_____

_____

_____

BLESSED BE THIS EVENING 🌙

Today I tried to be like Jesus by...

_____

A short prayer for someone:

_____

A short prayer for me:

_____

BIBLICAL KNOWLEDGE 💡

How did Elijah the Prophet mock Baal, the fake God of the Canaanites?

_____

_____

_____

_____

Today is: Su   M   T   W   Th   F   Sa

____ / ____ / _____

I thank God for...

1 _____

2 _____

3 _____

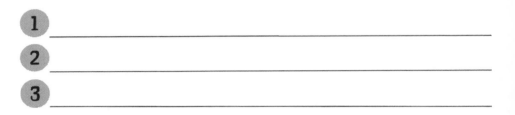

WRITE THIS BIBLE VERSE

HEBREWS 11:1

_____

_____

_____

_____

_____

_____

_____

BLESSED BE THIS EVENING 🌙

Today I tried to be like Jesus by...

_____

A short prayer for someone:

_____

A short prayer for me:

_____

BIBLICAL KNOWLEDGE 💡

What did Satan tell Eve would happen if she ate the forbidden fruit?

_____

_____

_____

_____

PRAISE GOD FOR THIS DAY

Today is: Su   M   T   W   Th   F   Sa

_____ / _____ / _____

I thank God for...

1 _____

2 _____

3 _____

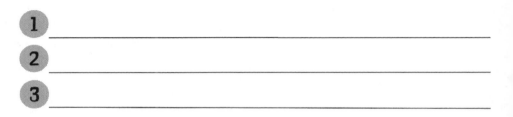

WRITE THIS BIBLE VERSE

REVELATION 21:4

_____

_____

_____

_____

_____

_____

_____

BLESSED BE THIS EVENING 🌙

Today I tried to be like Jesus by...

_____

A short prayer for someone:

_____

A short prayer for me:

_____

BIBLICAL KNOWLEDGE 💡

The word passion comes from the Latin word "passio" which means suffering. What is the Passion of Jesus?

_____

_____

_____

_____

PRAISE GOD FOR THIS DAY

Today is: Su M T W Th F Sa

____ / ____ / _____

I thank God for...

1 _____

2 _____

3 _____

WRITE THIS BIBLE VERSE

ROMANS 12:2

_____

_____

_____

_____

_____

_____

BLESSED BE THIS EVENING 🌙

Today I tried to be like Jesus by...

_____

A short prayer for someone:

_____

A short prayer for me:

_____

BIBLICAL KNOWLEDGE 💡

Noah was supposed to be the "new Adam". What did God ask Noah to do?

_____

_____

_____

_____

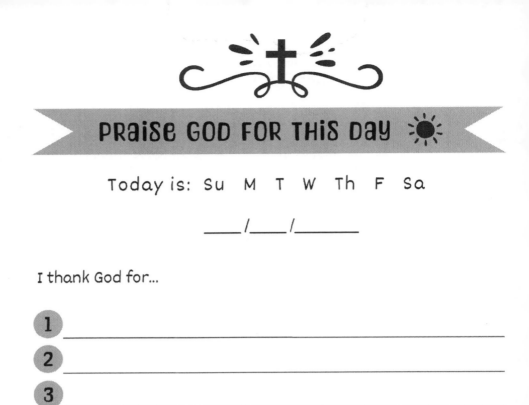

PRAISE GOD FOR THIS DAY

Today is: Su M T W Th F Sa

____ / ____ / _____

I thank God for...

1 _____

2 _____

3 _____

WRITE THIS BIBLE VERSE

PROVERBS 4:23

_____
_____
_____
_____
_____
_____
_____

BLESSED BE THIS EVENING 🌙

Today I tried to be like Jesus by...

_____

A short prayer for someone:

_____

A short prayer for me:

_____

BIBLICAL KNOWLEDGE 💡

What are two miracles that Jesus performed?

_____

_____

_____

_____

THANK YOU

FOR SUPPORTING A SMALL, CHRISTIAN-OWNED BUSINESS!

Please leave a review and let me know what you and your child think about this book. What did you like? What could be improved on? I'd love to know!

- Inel Williams

Made in the USA
Columbia, SC
20 May 2024

35956986R00072